Royal Blue Recollecti

Chris Harris

© Chris Harris 2017

All rights reserved. No part of this publication may be reproduced, stored in a retrieval system or transmitted, in any form or by any means, electronic, mechanical, photocopying, recording or otherwise, without prior permission in writing from Silver Link Publishing Ltd.

First published in 2017

British Library Cataloguing in Publication Data

A catalogue record for this book is available from the British Library.

ISBN 978 1 85794 506 5

Silver Link Publishing Ltd
The Trundle
Ringstead Road
Great Addington
Kettering
Northants NN14 4BW

Tel/Fax: 01536 330588
email: sales@nostalgiacollection.com
Website: www.nostalgiacollection.com

Printed and bound in the Czech Republic

Contents

Front cover: **BOURNEMOUTH** This evocative view perhaps encapsulates everything that was special about Royal Blue. On the left Bristol LL6B coach LTA 729, in service with Royal Blue from March 1951 until January 1964, lays over beside Bristol LS6B coach OTT 98, which was in the Royal Blue fleet from September 1953 until November 1969. Like the author, many readers of a certain age will have happy memories of Royal Blue coach journeys in both types of vehicle illustrated here. And thanks to the wonderful work done by preservationists, such an experience is still possible; LTA 729 is now owned by Colin Billington, while OTT 98 is in the care of the West Country Historic Omnibus & Transport Trust. Illustrating the care now lavished on these coaches, this photograph was taken during a Royal Blue staff reunion at the Heathlands Hotel, Bournemouth, on Thursday 9 May 2013. *Brian Jackson*

Title page: **TAUNTON** Parked between an Alder Valley coach on the left and a Shamrock & Rambler coach on the right, three Royal Blue coaches are seen during the summer of 1972 while taking a refreshment break at Taunton. From the left, RDV 443H, on its way to South Molton, Barnstaple and Ilfracombe, is a Bristol LH that had entered service with Royal Blue in 1970; Bristol MW6G 623 DDV, travelling to Bournemouth, was in service with Royal Blue from May 1960 until January 1976; while AEC Reliance 3MU3RU 938 GTA, on the way to Yeovil, had been new to Devon General in June 1961 and had transferred to the Royal Blue fleet in July 1971. *Brian Jackson collection*

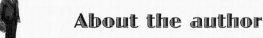

About the author

Chris Harris spent his career in the bus industry. He joined Hants & Dorset Motor Services Limited as a conductor at Poole depot back in the days when that company's buses were painted in Tilling green livery. After some years on the road, Chris was seconded to the Market Analysis Project in 1978, and later worked in Hants & Dorset's publicity department until the company was broken up in 1983. He then joined the Wilts & Dorset Bus Company, becoming Marketing Assistant in 1986 and Head of Marketing in 1993.

Chris remained in that role when the Go-Ahead Group bought Wilts & Dorset in 2003, and subsequently became Public Relations Manager for the Go South Coast family of companies in 2007, a position he held until his retirement a few years ago.

Since 1999 Chris has written a number of books covering transport history and local history, and derives great pleasure and satisfaction in doing so. Other interests and pleasures include walking in the countryside, literature and classical music. In retirement Chris still edits the Go South Coast staff magazine, and also edits *Wessex Review* for the Wessex Transport Society.

Rear cover: An interesting piece of Royal Blue advertising literature from 1924. The ornate fleet name is a delightful confection of artwork, with 'Pulchritudo et Salubritas' ('Beauty and Health') appropriated from the Bournemouth coat of arms. The vehicle illustrated is one of the earlier Daimler chars-a-banc that has been rebodied with a London Lorries all-weather body with side screens and a Beatonson hood, allowing it to become fully enclosed during inclement weather and creating a comfortable coach. The addition of pneumatic tyres and electric headlights, together with the introduction of a two-tone blue livery, significantly concealed the origins of the vehicle. *Andrew Waller collection*

Introduction

For many years Royal Blue was a general household word in South West England. It was used as a generic term for express coach travel; if anyone said they were going by Royal Blue, everyone knew that they would be making a journey by express coach.

With origins going back to 1887 when Thomas Elliott, at the age of 30, founded Royal Blue Mews in Avenue Lane, Bournemouth, Royal Blue developed to become one of the famous names in coach travel across a wide area of England. Having started in that year by hiring out horses and undertaking coachbuilding, saddling and blacksmith work, Elliott was soon offering a range of day trips and excursions from Bournemouth using horse-drawn chars-a-banc and coaches. Motor vehicles were introduced into the fleet by Elliott's sons in 1911, and the last horse-drawn carriages were withdrawn in 1914.

The stimulus of a railway strike in 1919 saw the introduction of an express coach service between Bournemouth and London, initially as an experimental summer weekend facility, but public demand was such that in 1921 this became a daily service. The motor coach fleet continued to expand, and in 1924 Royal Blue signed an agreement with Hants & Dorset Motor Services Limited that it would not operate any local bus services in the Bournemouth area, and in return Hants & Dorset would not operate coach tours and excursions.

The Tilling Group purchased Royal Blue from Elliott Brothers in January 1935. The excursions and tours side of the business was transferred to Hants & Dorset, which therefore ceased to be bound by the 1924 agreement. In 1935 Hants & Dorset started to use blue-liveried coaches and the name Royal Blue for tours and excursions but, no doubt to avoid confusion among potential customers, had repainted all the coaches in green and cream livery with the Hants & Dorset fleet name by the start of the 1937 season. Royal Blue's by then very extensive operation of express coach services was transferred to the joint control of Western National and Southern National. The Royal Blue name was retained for express coach operations, and the head office and management moved to the Western/Southern National headquarters in Queen Street, Exeter, although the major depot at Rutland Road, Bournemouth (established in 1920), was retained under the control of an engineering superintendent. There was also an operating superintendent based at the coach station in Exeter Road, Bournemouth, which had opened in 1931.

During the Second World War express coach services initially continued, but eventually had to be withdrawn in 1942 to conserve fuel. Nonetheless, a few long-distance limited-stop services were operated, serving corridors that did not have reasonable alternative rail and local bus links.

Post-war recovery began in 1946, and investment in new vehicles saw all pre-war coaches eliminated from the Royal Blue fleet in the spring of 1957. Passenger numbers continued to grow during the early 1950s; there was a setback later in that decade owing to the Suez crisis followed by a damaging strike in the middle of the 1957 summer season. Loadings had recovered by 1962, and peaked in 1965.

Royal Blue came under the control of the National Bus Company from 1 January 1969, and in 1970, perhaps as an indication of what was to come, coaches started to be painted in white with a dark blue waist-band. By 1973 the coaches had started to appear in the overall white National Express livery, which in due course signalled the end of Royal Blue as a brand. Much as the loss of this local identity is regretted, the National Express corporate identity was in many ways a master-stroke, driving home the message in all parts of the country that the company really was national.

It would not have been possible to have produced this book without the help that has been freely and kindly given by many people. Ian Gray, Peter Delaney, Colin Billington, John Weager, Norman Aish, Phil Duncan, Les Ronan, Roger Grimley, Phil Davies, Andrew Waller and David Pennels have all loaned material or provided vital snippets of information. I would like to especially thank *Brian Jackson* who most kindly sourced many of the photographs and also provided vital technical information and support. My thanks also to Peter Townsend and Will Adams at *The* NOSTALGIA *Collection* for their very kind help and support in publishing this book.

I hope you will enjoy this look back at the fondly remembered and well-loved coach operation that was Royal Blue.

Chris Harris
Poole, Dorset
May 2017

Elliott's Royal Blue

BOURNEMOUTH Thomas Elliott, a jobmaster, was only 30 years old in 1887 when he started the Royal Blue & Branksome Mews in Avenue Lane, Bournemouth. As this business developed, Mr Elliott developed a programme of excursions to places of interest around the Bournemouth area, and by the end of the 19th century destinations on offer included such delights as Lymington & Milford on Sea, Wimborne & Canford Park, and Sandbanks. Thomas was in due course joined in the business by his three sons, Jack, Harry and Ted. This photograph was taken in Christchurch Road just to the east of the Lansdowne on 26 August 1910; it shows a horse-drawn coach that has been cut down and adapted as a char-a-banc, with passengers dressed in their Edwardian finery ready to enjoy a trip to the New Forest. *Peter Delaney collection*

BOURNEMOUTH Thomas Elliott died in 1911, but the business continued to thrive, ably managed by his sons. In that year Royal Blue began to update to motor vehicles, and horse-drawn vehicles were finally eliminated from the fleet in 1914. Thus when horse-drawn brake No 23 was photographed on 21 August 1913 it only had a few months left before withdrawal. On the left of the photograph the tout appears to be spinning a yarn – indeed, over the years many facts of history have probably been 'enhanced' by enthusiastic coach drivers anticipating a good tip! *Peter Delaney collection*

Left: **BOURNEMOUTH** EL 1571 was the second of two Dennis 28hp chars-a-banc purchased in March 1913. Weighing 3 tons, these 20-seat vehicles were of solid construction, but note the wooden wheels – the spokes in these would often work loose, resulting in the wheels needing to be immersed in water overnight to tighten them up. Like a number of other operators, the Elliott brothers had purchased their early motor vehicles through a Government subsidy scheme that enabled them to be requisitioned in time of war. EL 1571 therefore only saw two summers of service in Bournemouth, where it was photographed on 28 July 1913. *Brian Jackson collection*

Below left: **BOURNEMOUTH** Photographed on 4 June 1914, before war changed the world for ever, on the right we see EL 1570, the other Dennis 28hp char-a-banc. Alongside is EL 2001, a 45hp Daimler, new in 1914 and the first in the fleet to be fitted with a 'Silent Knight' sleeve valve engine. On the plus side, this was economic in fuel and a quiet runner; its failing was that it used a considerable amount of lubricating oil and the valves required regular replacement. The 20-seat body by Ransom & Whitehead featured seating in three tiers to give all passengers a good view. By the time the war entered its third year EL 2001 had been sold to the Admiralty. *Brian Jackson collection*

Right: This is the very spartan basic cab layout of an early Daimler char-a-banc – the large handbrake is in the foreground, with the gate change gear lever close by. Note that the throttle pedal was placed between the clutch pedal and the footbrake. This represents a very different level of driver comfort compared with coaches a century later. *Brian Jackson collection*

Above: **BOURNEMOUTH** The first Daimler to join the Royal Blue fleet was EL 1833, which was delivered in July 1913. This was a 40hp vehicle powered by a Tylor engine. The vehicle's unladen weight was more than 4 tons, but it could achieve a fuel return of more than 7 miles per gallon. Access to the 26-seat body was by doors to each row of seats on the nearside only. Notice the smart crew in Royal Blue uniform. The company demanded a high standard – every driver had to be a trained mechanic as well as a skilled driver of exemplary character and a total abstainer. *Brian Jackson collection*

Left: **BOURNEMOUTH** Elliott's Royal Blue also operated a fleet of cars, which were advertised for hire for taxi journeys (e.g. to and from the theatre or to a railway station). This delightful period view shows one of Royal Blue's 16/24hp Unic taxis, illustrating the high-class service with liveried drivers. The vehicle is equipped with both oil and acetylene (carbide) lights. The tyre and rim on the running board was known as a Stepney wheel; in the event of a puncture it was simply strapped on to the outside of the offending wheel. *Brian Jackson collection*

Right: **BOURNEMOUTH** Royal Blue purchased 25 AEC Reliance 660 coaches in the first half of 1929. Lined up for a private hire at Bournemouth are (left to right) RU 8824, RU 8820, RU 8815 and RU 8801. Fitted with the A130 six-cylinder ohv petrol engine developing 95bhp, they were capable of reaching just over 40mph. The drive was via an inverted cone clutch to a four-speed gearbox mounted amidships. The accelerator was positioned between the footbrake and clutch pedal, and there was an inward curve to both the gate change gear lever and the handbrake, positioned side by side on the right of the cab. There were brakes on all four wheels, assisted by a single Dewandre servo. The 28-seat Duple bodies had a roll-back canvas roof (except RU 8815, which had 32 seats). In 1935 RU 8820 and RU 8824 went to Hants & Dorset, but were not taken into that operator's fleet, quickly passing via F. & E. Beedon of Towcester to United Counties before being withdrawn and sold for scrap in 1938. RU 8801 and RU 8815 passed to Southern National in 1935; the former received a 28-seat Beadle body in November of that year, but retained its petrol engine. *Brian Jackson collection*

Below: **BOURNEMOUTH** Lined up outside the Pavilion Theatre are five ADC type 424 and two Daimler CF6 models. From left to right we see RU 6721, RU 9031, RU 6731, RU 9035, RU 6722, RU 6725 and RU 6714. The ADC 424 models were delivered in 1928 and the Daimlers in 1929. RU 9031 had a 32-seat Duple body and passed to Southern National in 1935, being disposed of in 1938. RU 9035 had a 28-seat body by Duple and passed to Hants & Dorset in 1935; it was sold to Majestic Coaches of Bristol in 1937 and by May 1939 had passed to Avon Coaches of Netheravon, Wiltshire, finally being withdrawn in June 1950 following fire damage. *Brian Jackson collection*

Right: **BOURNEMOUTH** Six Daimler CF6 coaches with 28-seat Duple bodywork joined the Royal Blue fleet in June 1929, and four are seen in this line-up. In 1935 two coaches from this batch went to Hants & Dorset, and the other four to Western/Southern National. The leading vehicle, RU 9034, was one of those that went to Southern National, becoming its fleet number 3720. The National found that the six-cylinder sleeve valve engines were overdue for overhaul, and they were quickly replaced by AEC 7.7 units until these vehicles were disposed of (minus engines) in 1937-38. *Brian Jackson collection*

Below: **BOURNEMOUTH** An unusual two-tier bus and coach station was opened in Exeter Road, Bournemouth, in March 1931. Hants & Dorset bus services used the upper level, while Royal Blue coaches terminated in the basement. This photograph illustrates the unusual entrance and exit arrangements for vehicles using the lower level, with coaches entering on the right-hand side and coming out on the left; this situation applied until the premises were rebuilt in the late 1950s. Passengers used entrances in the side of the building. The vehicle entering is LJ 1511, a 1930 AEC Regal fitted with a two-door 28-seat Duple body. Note the local authority hackney plates still displayed on the rear – these had been a requirement before the 1930 Road Traffic Act. LJ 1511 passed to Southern National in 1935 (see also page 13). *Brian Jackson collection*

Right: **DOVER** In 1933-34 Royal Blue took delivery of four of the then very futuristic AEC Q coaches. LJ 8001, which arrived in August 1933, was the first vehicle of this type to be fitted with coach-type bodywork, by Duple with seats for 35 passengers. LJ 8600 and LJ 8601 followed in November 1933 and March 1934 respectively. The AEC 7.7-litre vertical engine (mounted in the traditional upright position) was located on the offside, outside of the chassis frame behind the front axle. During the summer of 1934 two of the AEC Q coaches were used to take members of the British Photographic Fellowship on a tour to Austria. In the days before drive-on drive-off ferries, vehicles had to be craned aboard; we can see LJ 8600 already safely stowed on the deck of SS *Forde* at Dover while LJ 8001 is suspended in mid-air. *Brian Jackson collection*

BOURNEMOUTH In February 1935 the Tilling Association acquired the Royal Blue coach operation from Elliott Brothers of Bournemouth. Royal Blue's express coach services passed to Western and Southern National, while private hire, excursions and tours came to Hants & Dorset. The Royal Blue vehicles were transferred, 36 to Western National, 35 to Southern National and 38 to Hants & Dorset. Also taken over by Hants & Dorset was the leasehold of 8 Bath Road, Bournemouth, which was being used by Royal Blue at that time. These premises are seen just after the transfer to Hants & Dorset, with the fourth AEC Q, AEL 2, new to Royal Blue in June 1934, standing on the forecourt. This differed from the previous three Qs by having a Harrington body. All four of the AEC Q coaches went to Hants & Dorset, where they remained in service until 1949, while the Bath Road premises were to become the Registered Office of Hants & Dorset Motor Services between 1948 and 1958. We will continue the story of the services operated under the Royal Blue name by Western National and Southern National in the following chapters. *Brian Jackson collection*

Into Tilling – and the Second World War

The shape of Bristol JJW ETA 453, new in March 1935 with a 32-seat Eastern Counties body, clearly indicates the style of future Tilling coaches. The polished hammered aluminium bonnet side adds to the generally smart appearance afforded by the dark blue livery. Notice the Royal Blue fleet name on the side with a central emblem showing the fleet number (163) within a circular Western National device – a short-lived design that was soon to be replaced by the familiar 'winged wheel'. During part of the Second World War ETA 453 was converted to run on producer gas, then in 1949 it was fitted with a Gardner 5LW engine and given a new Beadle 36-seat bus body, thereafter being used on local Western National bus services until withdrawn in 1958. *Brian Jackson collection*

Above: **RIVER DART** It is impossible to put a price on good publicity, and nobody knew this better than Mr Clement Preece, Traffic Superintendent (Express Services), who arranged this photograph during the summer of 1939 using holidaymakers given a free day out by coach provided that they were happy for publicity photographs to be taken along the way. AEC Regal LJ 1519 looks immaculate, having just received a new 32-seat Beadle coach body in May of that year. In the background is the River Dart above Kingswear, with troopships at anchor; the re-touch artist has made them look attractive and also transformed some of the weeds in the foreground into more attractive flowers. The superb photograph that resulted was used in Royal Blue publicity material for a number of years after the war. Unfortunately LJ 1519 was severely damaged during an air raid in August 1943 and subsequently broken up for scrap in 1944. *Brian Jackson collection*

Right: **BRIDPORT** Royal Blue express coach services continued to run during the early years of the Second World War, often carrying very heavy loads under extremely difficult conditions. The blackout regulations would have made driving a large vehicle full of passengers at night particularly stressful; note the masked headlamps and white-painted mudguard tips of AEC Regal ETA 996, photographed at Bridport during 1942. This coach had been new in 1937 and is carrying a 32-seat Duple body fitted in April 1941 to replace the original Duple example, which had been destroyed in a fire near Tidworth late in 1939. ETA 996 was withdrawn in 1956 and sold to Halford of Torquay, becoming a racing car transporter. *The late David Habgood collection*

Right: **SOMEWHERE IN SOUTHERN ENGLAND** In November 1942, as a result of the very serious fuel situation, all Royal Blue express coach services had to cease. However, a number of cross-country routes were identified that were not adequately served by the railway network or local bus services. Authorisation was given for the introduction of several limited-stop stage carriage (i.e. bus) services that were in fact provided by using Royal Blue coaches. One such route was the 405 from Bournemouth to Warminster and Trowbridge. AEC Regal ETA 983, carrying a 31-seat Mumford coach body and new in 1937, is seen operating on route 405 under wartime conditions. After the war ETA 983 was fitted with a 31-seat Beadle coach body and continued in Royal Blue service until withdrawn in 1957, passing to Comberhill Motors (dealer) of Wakefield, then to Gillard of Normanton. *The late David Habgood collection*

Post-war recovery and halcyon days

BRISTOL Following the end of the Second World War in 1945, Royal Blue express coach services resumed operation in April 1946. In the austere post-war conditions new coaches were not available, and the pre-war coaches returned to their old duties, forming the backbone of the fleet for the next couple of years. This photograph, taken outside the Bristol Tramways & Carriage Company's offices in Princes Street, illustrates vehicles available in the immediate post-war period. Leading is Royal Blue ATT 938, a 1935 Bristol JJW with a Weymann coach body. Subsequently this vehicle was re-bodied by Beadle in 1948 as a 36-seat bus and joined the Southern National fleet; withdrawn in 1958, it was sold to a showman in Dorchester and not broken up until the winter of 1973-74. Following ATT 938 in this photograph is a Black & White Motorways Bristol JO6G dating from 1937, which in turn is followed by a Yelloways Bedford/Duple coach. *Brian Jackson collection*

LONDON When photographed in the early post-war period while still carrying its original Eastern Counties 32-seat coach body, 1935 Bristol JJW BTA 460 in all honesty looks rather tired. This is not surprising, as it was one of the 17 Royal Blue vehicles that had been modified to run on producer gas during the war; the performance of these converted vehicles was very poor, and all concerned were pleased when the scheme was abandoned. BTA 460 was also subsequently rebodied by Beadle as a single-deck bus, and gave a further ten years service in this capacity before withdrawal and sale to an Aldershot showman in 1958. *Brian Jackson collection*

LONDON In a photograph that really captures the atmosphere of holiday journeys by Royal Blue in the early post-war period, families can be seen beside DR 8638, which has operated a relief journey to London. This Leyland TS1 had started life as a coach in the Western National fleet in May 1931, and was rebodied by Beadle for the Royal Blue fleet in 1939. Notice the Royal Blue plate on the 'Cov-Rad' radiator. DR 8638 remained in the fleet until January 1953. *Brian Jackson collection*

LONDON On page 8 we saw 1930-built AEC Regal LJ 1511 carrying its original two-door 28-seat Duple body and entering the new Bournemouth coach station in 1931. Here is a post-war photograph of the same coach, which had been given a new Beadle 32-seat coach body in 1936. This coach remained in the Royal Blue fleet until it was sold to a dealer in Cardiff in October 1953. *Andrew Waller collection*

AEC Reliance RU 8807 had carried a Duple two-door 28-seat coach body when it was new to Elliott Brothers in 1929. It was allocated to the Southern National Royal Blue fleet in January 1935, and received a new Beadle 28-seat coach body in November of that year. To accommodate the new body on the short chassis, a slight variation of the standard Royal Blue pattern was fitted; note the small window above the 'winged wheel' logo in the middle of the fleet name. RU 8807 was withdrawn from Royal Blue service in November 1949 and sold to Bowers of Chard (breakers). *R. H. G. Simpson*

OXFORD Leyland TS1 TR 9922 had been new in 1931, and joined the Royal Blue fleet in May 1935 with the acquisition of Tourist Coaches of Southampton. It is seen here at Gloucester Green, Oxford, in the early 1950s, carrying the 31-seat Beadle coach body it had been given in 1939. The Royal Blue plate on the 'Cov-Rad' radiator will be noted. TR 9922 remained in Royal Blue service until March 1954, when it was sold for scrap. *R. H. G. Simpson*

OXFORD New to Elliott Brothers in June 1930, AEC Reliance LJ 1525 became part of the Southern National Royal Blue fleet after acquisition in 1935. It was photographed towards the end of its service at Oxford, carrying the 32-seat Beadle coach body it had received in December 1935. It was sold out of service in January 1954; a surviving note records that the diesel engine was removed at Bournemouth prior to the sale. Of equal interest is the coach on the left of this view. VRF 630 was a Leyland PSU1/12 Royal Tiger that had been new to Harper Brothers of Heath Hayes in 1951; the 41-seat centre-entrance coach body is by Metalcraft of Staffordshire, a company formed in 1946 that built a total of 110 bodies for buses and coaches before production ceased early in 1954. *Brian Jackson collection*

NEWBURY Three Royal Blue coaches are photographed during a refreshment break at The Wharf, Newbury, in August 1950. On the left HOD 104, bound for Birmingham, is a Bristol L6B carrying a 31-seat coach body by Duple; this vehicle was in service with Royal Blue from September 1949 until April 1960. In the middle AEC Reliance ETA 993 is operating as a relief car to Birmingham; this coach was in the Royal Blue fleet for 20 years from 1937 until 1957, and had received a new Beadle front-entrance coach body in 1949 by the time this photograph was taken. On the right, operating a relief journey to Coventry, Bristol L6B JUO 935 had been new to Royal Blue in June 1948 and carried a 31-seat Beadle coach body; this was subsequently removed and the chassis lengthened to allow the fitting of a new Eastern Coach Works bus body; this vehicle then served for more than ten years as a driver-only-operated bus on local routes in the West Country. *L. Ronan collection*

ALDERSHOT Two Bristol L6B coaches carrying 31-seat bodies by Beadle are seen picking up passengers at Aldershot bus station while operating on Associated Motorways journeys. Closest to the camera and on its way to Portsmouth, HOD 103 was new in August 1949, but was to see less than 11 years of service with Royal Blue, being withdrawn in April 1960 and scrapped by Rundle (breaker) of Plymouth. Following behind and heading for Southampton, JUO 987 had been new to the Royal Blue fleet in September 1948; it served as a coach until 1958, when it was given a new Eastern Coach Works bus body and in this guise was used on local routes in the West Country for almost another 12 years until withdrawn in 1970. Notice the fashions of the early 1950s worn by the passengers boarding HOD 103. *R. Blencowe collection*

HENLEY-ON-THAMES Associated Motorways was a partnership and pool of express coach operators who worked together to advertise coach services covering a large area of the country. A major coordination scheme that was of great benefit to coach travellers, Associated Motorways first came into being in 1934; in addition to Royal Blue, the original members included Black & White Motorways, BMMO (Midland Red), Greyhound Motor Services, Red & White, and United Counties. Crosville, Eastern Counties and Lincolnshire Road Car later joined the pool, which remained until the routes in question became part of the National Express network in the early 1970s. Royal Blue Bristol L6B coach JUO 944, new in August 1948, was photographed in Henley-on-Thames in 1951 while operating on the Associated Motorways route from Portsmouth to Birmingham via Aldershot, Oxford and Coventry. *L. Ronan collection*

HARTLEY WINTNEY For many years the Swan Hotel at Hartley Wintney was a refreshment stop for Royal Blue coaches travelling along the A30 road south-west of London. This photograph, taken in the early 1950s, could be described as 'ancient and modern'. On the right is DR 8882, a Leyland TS2 that had been new to Western National in 1931 with a 26-seat Mumford coach body. It was transferred to the Royal Blue fleet in 1935 and given a new 32-seat Beadle coach body in 1939. It was withdrawn in January 1953. On the left is Bristol L6B LTA 727, which had entered service in September 1950 and was thus nearly new when this photograph was taken. Carrying a 33-seat coach body by Duple, LTA 727 had a very short service life, being withdrawn and scrapped in November 1961. Notice the smart clothing of the couple deep in conversation beside LTA 727; a gentleman would have considered a suit to be very appropriate apparel for a coach journey in the 1950s. *L. Ronan collection*

NEWBURY An express coach service between Southampton and Liverpool had been started by Tourist Coaches of Southampton in June 1930, and in 1933 the southern terminal of this long route was extended to Bournemouth. After Tourist became part of the Tilling organisation in 1935, its express services were absorbed into the Royal Blue network; the Bournemouth-Southampton-Liverpool route in due course became part of the Associated Motorways pool in 1938, with Royal Blue retaining operating control. Duple-bodied Bristol L6B LTA 888 was photographed operating between Bournemouth and Liverpool in June 1951; Portsmouth would have been served by a connecting coach at Southampton. *L. Ronan collection*

Below & left: **HENDON** In 1950 the Ministry of Transport announced that public service vehicles registered after 1 June that year could be up to 30 feet long – previously the limit had been 27ft 6in. Royal Blue was quick to take advantage of the extra seating capacity that this additional length could provide, and ordered a batch of 24 Bristol LL6B coaches with 37-seat coach bodies by Duple, and they entered service in March and May 1951. Seen brand new outside the Duple factory at Hendon in March 1951, this batch of coaches is exemplified by LTA 734.

The interior view shows the high standard of accommodation aboard these fine coaches, which many people regarded as being the most attractive of all of the types operated by Royal Blue. This batch of coaches remained in Royal Blue service until 1963-64. *Both L. Ronan collection*

Above: **WEYMOUTH** A service van was used to move small stores to depots, and to keep the various booking offices and agents supplied with up-to-date publicity material – together with a host of miscellaneous tasks necessary to keep the wheels turning smoothly and promote the business. One vehicle used in this unsung, but vital, role was VYC 38, an Austin A40 van new in 1955 and photographed at Weymouth garage in September 1956. VYC 38 was in use with the company until 1962. *Brian Jackson*

MARLBOROUGH The picturesque Wiltshire town of Marlborough is on the old A4 trunk road from London to Bath and Bristol. It boasts the second widest High Street in England (the widest is at Stockton-on-Tees). A motor coach service between London and Bristol via Marlborough had been started by Greyhound Motors in 1925 and in the 1930s this became a joint operation involving Royal Blue and the Bristol Tramways & Carriage Company; it lasted until 1965 when the Bristol company took over the complete working of the service. On this occasion in the early 1950s Royal Blue Bristol L6A coach HOD 102 is seen during a refreshment break in Marlborough High Street while working as a relief car on a journey to Cheltenham. New in March 1949, HOD 102 was in service with Royal Blue until April 1960. *L. Ronan collection*

LONDON When Leyland TS2 UU 1566 was photographed at Victoria coach station in London during the early 1950s it was nearing the end of its days with Royal Blue. New to Western National in May 1929, this vehicle was given a new 26-seat coach body by Beadle in 1937 and transferred to the Royal Blue fleet. It will be noticed that a 'Cov-Rad' radiator has been fitted; these were often used on re-bodied vehicles to give the impression of a younger machine, although this is perhaps a case of beauty being in the eye of the beholder. UU 1566 was withdrawn and scrapped in 1953. *R. H. G. Simpson*

WEYMOUTH This photograph, taken in the early 1950s, shows 1937 AEC Regal ETA 996 in the remains of the bus garage at Edward Street, Weymouth. These premises had been destroyed by bombing in 1940; rebuilding commenced in late 1954 and was not fully completed until April 1956. As mentioned on page 11, the coach's original Duple body had been destroyed in a fire near Tidworth in late 1939, and it was given the replacement Duple body seen here in 1941. The new body was of a more streamlined appearance, and set the standard for post-war examples. ETA 996 was withdrawn in 1956 and sold to Halford of Torquay, in due course being converted to a racing car transporter. *R. H. G. Simpson*

OXFORD This excellent, detailed view of the doorway and nearside of Bristol L6B JUO 934 at Gloucester Green, Oxford, illustrates the first impression of their coach that would await Royal Blue passengers in the early 1950s. The 31-seat Beadle coach body was as comfortable as it was visually inviting, and Royal Blue coach services were held in very high esteem by their clientele. JUO 934 had been new in June 1948, but served only 10 years as a Royal Blue coach; in 1958 it was given a new Eastern Coach Works bus body, which was modified to be suitable for operation over the Torpoint ferry. It was used as a Western National bus until March 1969, when it became a mobile office at Newquay until sold to a dealer in November of that year. It passed to Evans of Washington, Durham, in April 1970, and was finally withdrawn and broken up in 1977. *R. H. G. Simpson*

BRISTOL For many years the Associated Motorways network was based on a hub at Cheltenham, where routes from various parts of the country connected to provide passengers with a very wide range of journey opportunities involving just the one change of coach. Bristol LL6B LTA 898 was photographed at Princes Street in Bristol while working a service from Plymouth to Cheltenham in the early 1950s. LTA 898 was in service with Royal Blue from March 1951 until February 1964. *L. Ronan collection*

EXETER This scene at the congested Paul Street bus and coach station in Exeter dates from June 1952. Bristol L6B coaches JUO 932 and JUO 987 are preparing to depart with feeder services to Newquay and Falmouth. Both of these coaches were new in 1948; JUO 932 was one of the first new coaches to be received by Royal Blue after the Second World War. By the end of the 1950s the bus and coach station at Paul Street was no longer adequate, and a new bus and coach station was opened in Paris Street in 1964; no trace now remains of the Paul Street premises, the site being occupied by part of the Harlequin shopping centre. *L. Ronan collection*

JULY 1952 saw the introduction of the first Bristol LS6G coaches into the Royal Blue fleet. Of semi-integral construction, these had their six-cylinder Gardner engines mounted under the floor in the middle of the coach and the full-fronted body was therefore able to provide seating for 41 passengers. LTA 867 was the first of the batch to enter service with Royal Blue, and is seen when new while operating on the route from Portsmouth to Liverpool for Associated Motorways – a trip that took just 10 minutes under 12 hours in 1952. Early Bristol LS coaches had the attractive curved corner glass at the front of the vehicle, but at night these were found to give distracting reflections to drivers. Notice the outward opening door and the traditional roof pannier for luggage. *Brian Jackson collection*

SOUTHAMPTON First licensed by Royal Blue in August 1953, Bristol LS6G OTT 44 was almost new when photographed at Grosvenor Square, Southampton, while operating a service to London on 7 September 1953. Note the revised design of the windscreen compared with LTA 867 in the previous photograph – perhaps less aesthetically appealing, but certainly much safer and more practical. The outward-opening door and the roof luggage area continued to be specified; close inspection will also reveal the fitting of semaphore-type traffic indicators above the front wheel arch. OTT 44 was in service with Royal Blue until 1969, later passing into preservation. In the background a Duple-bodied Bedford OB from the Southern National fleet is providing a relief car for the London service. *The late R. B. Gosling*

BOURNEMOUTH AEC Regal ETA 976 had been new to Royal Blue in 1937 and had originally carried a Mumford coach body; this was replaced in 1949 by the 31-seat Beadle coach body seen in this photograph, which was taken beside Bournemouth bus and coach station on 1 August 1953. ETA 976 awaits the call to duty to provide a relief car to Southampton. This coach was in service with Royal Blue for 20 years, and after withdrawal in 1957 it passed to Camberhill Motors (dealers) of Wakefield, who later sold it to Gillards of Normanton for further service. *The late R. B. Gosling*

HARTLEY WINTNEY Bristol LL6B LTA 900 is seen during an early evening refreshment break at the Swan Inn in Hartley Wintney during 1953. Having left Exmouth at 8.45am, via Seaton (10.01am) and Weymouth (noon) to Bournemouth (lunch break; arrive 1.28pm, depart 3.00pm), the time is now about 6.00pm with a scheduled arrival at London Victoria coach station at 7.56pm. The fare for this journey in 1953 was £1 2s 3d single or £1 19s 6d period return. On the right of the photograph we see HUU 726, a Duple-bodied Bedford OB of Tilling Transport (BTC) Limited, which was on hire to Royal Blue as a relief. *L. Ronan collection*

Left: Shortly after the fleet had been acquired by Western/Southern National, a new emblem graced the sides of vehicles. It consisted of a winged and dust-trailed wheel, with 'N' in the centre. Either 'Western National' or 'Southern National' encircled the rim of the wheel, and the device was flanked by 'ROYAL BLUE' on the supporting lozenge. It was used until the 1960s, by which time it was regarded as outdated. *Stuart Andrews*

YEOVIL For many years the forecourt of Yeovil Town station was a significant interchange point for Royal Blue coach services. This photograph was taken on 9 April 1954, and on the left we see LTA 736, a Bristol LL6B new in 1951, withdrawn in 1963 and broken up by Rundle of Plymouth in February 1965. In the centre is LTA 871, a Bristol LS6G new to Royal Blue in 1952 and in service until 1968; it later saw a couple of years further use in the ownership of Shephardson of Barton-on-Humber. On the right is LTA 968, a 1951 Bristol LL6B that was withdrawn in 1963. Yeovil Town station was closed to passengers from 3 October 1966; for some years thereafter there was a car park on the site, but a cinema and leisure complex has now been built in this location and there is little indication of its former importance as a public transport hub. *The late R. B. Gosling*

BOURNEMOUTH This mid-1950s photograph nicely illustrates Royal Blue coaches arriving at and departing from the unusual two-tier bus and coach station in Bournemouth before it was extensively rebuilt in 1957-59. On the right is Bristol LS6G MOD 978 descending the ramp to the basement-level coach station; this coach was new in September 1952 and withdrawn in July 1968. On the left, Bristol LS6G OTT 92, which had entered service in August 1953, is departing with a service to Totnes. The ramp up to the Hants & Dorset bus station can be seen in the centre of the photograph. *John Weager collection*

CHICHESTER Operated jointly by Royal Blue, Southdown and East Kent, the through coach service between Bournemouth and Margate was marketed as the South Coast Express. In 1954 the end-to-end journey took more than 12 hours, leaving Bournemouth at 8.35am and arriving at Margate at 9.06pm. Along the way there were refreshment stops at Hilsea, Brighton (an extended stop of 1hr 15min to allow for lunch), Hastings and Hythe. Here we see Bristol LS6G OTT 93 in West Street, Chichester, during the journey in June 1954. On the opposite side of the road a Southdown Leyland TD5 is picking up passengers for Selsey, and just visible in the distance an Aldershot & District Dennis Lancet has arrived with the service from Aldershot to Bognor Regis via Haslemere. *L. Ronan collection*

READING The side destination blinds on Bristol L6A HOD 102, photographed at the Colonnade coach station, Reading, in 1953, clearly show that this coach is operating the Associated Motorways service at 1.10pm from Oxford to Portsmouth via Reading, Basingstoke, Winchester (refreshment stop), Southampton and Fareham; arrival at Portsmouth will be at 5.42pm. New in March 1949, HOD 102 was in service with Royal Blue until April 1960. *L. Ronan collection*

NEWBURY For some years a popular refreshment stop on routes to and from the Midlands and the North, this photograph was taken at The Wharf, Newbury, in July 1954. On the left Bristol L6B LTA 727, new in September 1950, is operating the Liverpool to Southampton route, while beside it is Bristol L6A HOD 101, new in February 1949, operating as a relief car and running through to Bournemouth. The route between Southampton and Liverpool was inherited from Tourist Coaches in 1935; the link between these two important cities was originally conceived for the benefit of the shipping community. *L. Ronan collection*

LONDON Between 1953 and 1957 a total of 66 Bedford OB coaches operated by Southern National and Western National had their erstwhile green-painted areas replaced by dark blue and they were given Royal Blue fleet names. It was intended that these vehicles would bring passengers from some of the smaller resorts to connectional hubs (such as Exeter) where they would change onto a larger coach for their onward journey. Such was the volume of coach traffic in the mid-1950s that these Bedford OBs often found their way to London on relief journeys; LTA 925 was photographed after arrival at Victoria coach station as passengers collect their luggage at the end of this stage of their journey. *Brian Jackson collection*

FALMOUTH An unusual Bedford OB to be given Royal Blue colours and fleet names was KAF 110. This vehicle had been new to Selene Coaches (Banfil & Barrington) of Mawnan Smith, Falmouth, Cornwall, whose services were taken over by Western National from 12 November 1953. It is somewhat surprising that KAF 110 was subsequently given Royal Blue livery and fleet names for, as a close examination of the photograph will prove, it was fitted with bus, rather than coach, seats. It was also the only Royal Blue-liveried Bedford OB to carry a Thurgood body; the other 65 OBs thus redesignated all carried bodies by Duple. KAF 110 only spent a short time as a Royal Blue vehicle, being withdrawn in 1955 and passing to a dealer in Wakefield. In February 1956 it was sold to the Cyprus Transport Company of Nicosia where, reregistered as TW 579, it gave a further 15 years service before finally being withdrawn in June 1971 – a great demonstration of the durability of the Bedford OB. *Norman Aish collection*

HENLEY-ON-THAMES The 30-foot-long Bristol LL6B coaches introduced in 1951 were considered by many to have been the most distinguished and elegant coaches operated by Royal Blue. LTA 736 was photographed while operating on an Associated Motorways journey to Walsall via Aldershot and Oxford, and certainly presents a very inviting yet purposeful impression to the potential traveller. It is clearly a warm summer day, and passengers have opened most of the wind-down side windows. LTA 736 carried a 37-seat body by Duple and was in service with Royal Blue from May 1951 until February 1964. *Brian Jackson collection*

SOUTHAMPTON Until the autumn of 1955 Royal Blue coaches had picked up in Grosvenor Square in Southampton, but from September of that year the calling point was moved to the coach station in Bedford Place, effectively on the other side of the Hants & Dorset bus garage. Southampton was an important boarding and interchange point for Royal Blue and Associated Motorways passengers, and this photograph shows Bristol LL6B LTA 894, new in March 1951, calling with the 2.15pm journey from Portsmouth (Hyde Park Road) to Bournemouth in 1958, three years after these express coach routes started to call at Bedford Place; the coach station was subsequently closed in 1988 and no trace of it remains in the 21st century. The present National Express coach station in the city at Harbour Parade was opened in 1999. *L. Ronan collection*

WESTON-SUPER-MARE Photographed during August 1956, closest to the camera we see Royal Blue Bristol LS6G OTT 97, new in September 1953, waiting to depart with the 4.30pm service to London via Chippenham and Newbury. Next to OTT 97, Royal Blue Bristol L6B JUO 986, new in September 1948, will provide the 5.00pm service to Bournemouth via Bridgwater, Yeovil and Blandford. The Willowbrook-bodied Guy UF operated by Black & White, seen on the extreme left of the photograph, will in due course depart for Cheltenham. *L. Ronan collection*

SOUTHAMPTON The Bristol LS6G coaches delivered to Royal Blue in 1953 were the last to feature the roof luggage container reached by fold-down chromium steps on the rear of the coach. A change to the Royal Blue livery saw the roofs of the coaches painted cream from 1958 onwards, and this photograph taken at Bedford Place, Southampton, in the rather wet autumn of that year compares the old and new paint schemes when seen from the rear. On the left, 1951 Bristol LL6B LTA 894, operating a Portsmouth to Bournemouth service, retains the traditional blue roof, while on the right 1953 Bristol LS6B OTT 98 has been repainted in the new style. The latter was the last Royal Blue coach to be delivered with a roof luggage container, and happily survives in preservation (see front cover and pages 36 & 47). *L. Ronan collection*

MAIDENHEAD Photographed in June 1958 while operating a journey to Weston-super-Mare via Newbury and Chippenham, Bristol LL6B LTA 967 is seen at Maidenhead coach station. After 1963 express coaches called at the bus station rather than at this facility. Carrying a 37-seat body by Duple, LTA 967 was new in May 1951 and sold in February 1964. *L. Ronan collection*

LONDON Having left their suitcases at the rear of the coach for the driver to stow on board, two ladies – fashionably dressed for the coach journey – are making for Bristol LL6B LTA 969, which will shortly depart as a relief car to Bournemouth. This coach entered service with Royal Blue in May 1951 and was in the fleet until February 1964. On the right of the photograph, Bristol LS6G VDV 772, new in April 1957, has just arrived from Bournemouth with a service routed via Guildford. *L. Ronan collection*

HENLEY-ON-THAMES Traffic was busy during the warm and settled summer of 1959 when Bristol MW6G XUO 717 was photographed passing through Henley-on-Thames while operating the 9.30am Birmingham to Portsmouth service. Examination of the photograph shows two other Royal Blue coaches going in the other direction, heading towards the Market Place pick-up point – a Bristol MW6G is leading a Bristol LL6B, the latter still sporting the traditional-style blue roof. *L. Ronan collection*

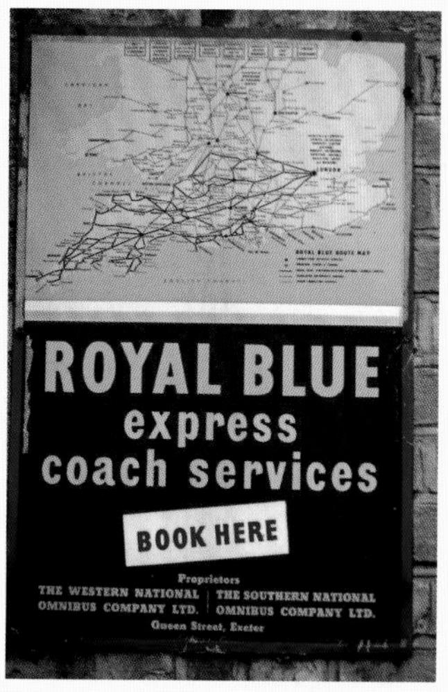

Right: **ROYAL BLUE** booking agents were supplied with these eye-catching metal signs that were fitted to the exterior of their premises. The convenience of a local booking agent and pick-up point ensured that many people chose to travel by express coach. *David Pennels*

TOTNES Bristol LS6G MOD 975, new to Royal Blue in July 1952, was certainly well loaded when it was caught by the camera awaiting departure time from outside the Western National booking office at The Plains, Totnes, in May 1960. At that time the fare for this journey was £1 10s 6d single and £2 14s 0d period return. MOD 975 was in the Royal Blue fleet until April 1967. *L. Ronan collection*

CHICHESTER After entering service with Royal Blue in June 1961, Bristol MW6G 59 GUO is seen in August of that year at Chichester bus station waiting for the 12.05pm departure time while operating the through service from Bournemouth to Margate, where it will arrive at 8.27pm, having given passengers a grand tour of the South Coast. Note the 'South Coast Express' label in the nearside windscreen, which also indicates that the service is operated jointly by East Kent, Royal Blue and Southdown. *L. Ronan collection*

LOOE Bristol LL6B LTA 729 was parked at Looe, Cornwall, when this photograph was taken in August 1962. This offside rear three-quarter view illustrates very clearly the folding chrome-plated steps leading up to the roof luggage container, which was a standard fitment on Royal Blue coaches delivered up to and including 1953. Both the steps and the chrome hand rail could become extremely slippery on a wet day; lifting heavy cases onto the rack could be quite an ordeal for the driver and a good degree of physical strength was required. New in 1951, LTA 729 was withdrawn after the 1963 season and passed to Somerset operator Sherrin of Carhampton, and later to Richards of Spaxton. In the 21st century it has been beautifully restored in the ownership of Colin Billington (see front cover). *L. Ronan collection*

CHICHESTER In 1962 the Eastern Coach Works coach body fitted to the Bristol MW chassis was given a revised design; one feature that passengers noticed at once was that the destination screens had been moved from the front dome to below the windscreen. New to Royal Blue in June 1963 and illustrating the new style, 746 MDV was only a few weeks old when caught by the camera in Chichester bus station during August of that year while operating the 8.25am journey from Bournemouth to Brighton on the South Coast Express route. *L. Ronan collection*

FALMOUTH Royal Blue ran regular services to Helston, where Western National had an office in Coinagehall Street and a garage in Clodgey Lane. There were also summer-only extensions of the service onwards to Porthleven. Bound for Helston, Bristol LS6G MOD 979 was quite close to the end of its journey when it was photographed at The Moor, Falmouth. It was in service with Royal Blue from 1952 until 1968. *L. Ronan collection*

THE WESTERN NATIONAL OMNIBUS COMPANY LIMITED — PROPRIETORS OF — THE SOUTHERN NATIONAL OMNIBUS COMPANY LIMITED

ROYAL BLUE

EXPRESS SERVICES

TELEGRAMS: NATCARCOM, EXETER

TELEPHONE NO. EXETER 4191

MEMBERS OF ASSOCIATED MOTORWAYS

HEAD OFFICE: 48/50, QUEEN STREET EXETER

YOUR REF.

OUR REF. 3/0/3

HARTLEY WINTNEY A welcome innovation was the introduction of seasonal journeys between London and Bournemouth routed via Hurn Airport to connect with flights to and from the Channel Islands operated by Jersey Airlines/British United Airways. Introduced in the late 1950s, this service was very popular in the mid-1960s. Bristol LS6G VDV 776 is taking a 15-minute refreshment break at the Swan Hotel, Hartley Wintney, while operating the 10.00 London to Bournemouth via Hurn Airport journey in July 1964. *L. Ronan collection*

PENZANCE The coach journey from London to Penzance took more than 12 hours, but included a number of refreshment breaks along the way. In this photograph, taken at Penzance around 1960, we see VDV 777, new to Royal Blue in May 1957 and the last Bristol LS6G coach to be taken into stock. To the right is a Bedford OB coach liveried for Royal Blue work, and used mostly on more local duties. *Brian Jackson collection*

LITTLEHAMPTON The South Coast Express route, operated jointly by Royal Blue, East Kent and Southdown, was a very convenient link between the Sussex coastal towns and Bournemouth. Bristol MW6G 747 MDV, new to Royal Blue in 1963, was photographed picking up passengers travelling towards Southampton and Bournemouth at Littlehampton on 27 March 1966. *Brian Jackson collection*

WINCHESTER Making the first of several refreshment stops on its 12-hour journey from Bournemouth to Liverpool, operated for Associated Motorways, Royal Blue Bristol MW6G 764 MDV was caught by the camera at Worthy Lane coach station, Winchester, in August 1964. Passengers travelling long distances by coach obviously require refreshment breaks from time to time during the journey, and these halts resulted in a coach-load of people descending all together on a café and requiring to be served in the minimum of time so that the coach could keep to schedule. The ideal situation was a café within a coach station, as here at Winchester, where the proprietor understood the particular needs of catering for passengers in these circumstances. *L. Ronan collection*

WINCHESTER A particular landmark in the Worthy Lane coach station was the controllers' tower, which also incorporated a Royal Blue booking office on the ground floor. The distinctive structure can be seen on the right of this photograph, which shows Bristol MW6G 621 DDV laying over at the coach station while its passengers partake of refreshment during the 15-minute break. New to Royal Blue in March 1960, 621 DDV was subsequently converted to a driver-only-operated bus in 1973 and was with Western National in this capacity until October 1978, when it was sold to Hartwood Exports. Express coach services ceased using Worthy Lane coach station in 1980 and now pick up and set down at stops in Winchester Broadway. In 2017 the Winchester Hotel occupies much of the site of the erstwhile coach station. *Brian Jackson*

BIDEFORD The National Omnibus & Transport Company had acquired premises beside the River Torridge at Bideford in 1927. The spacious site effectively became a major engineering works for Western National following the severe bombing of Plymouth during the Second World War. This role continued for many years after the war, with many Royal Blue coaches receiving attention here. On the left is Bristol LS6G OTT 98. New in September 1953, it was subsequently withdrawn in April 1970 and passed to H&C Coaches of Garston before being acquired for preservation by the Dorset Transport Circle in 1972; at the time of writing it is in the care of John Grigg of Portishead (see also front cover). On the right, VDV 746, new in 1957, was the first Bristol LS6G to be delivered to Royal Blue without the traditional luggage container. After withdrawal in 1970, VDV 746 passed to Morris of Swansea until scrapped in 1976. Riverside Works was demolished in 1989. *The late David Habgood*

BOURNEMOUTH With the purchase of Royal Blue from Elliott Brothers in 1935 came premises at Rutland Road in the Charminster suburb of Bournemouth. Originally acquired by Elliott Brothers in 1921, these premises consisted of three sheds that had been built for aircraft production. During the winter period around 25 per cent of the Royal Blue fleet was stored at Rutland Road, and this photograph, taken during the late 1960s, shows a number of Bristol MW coaches hibernating there, awaiting their return to service with the spring timetable uplift. Express coaches ceased to use Rutland Road depot in the late 1970s. *The late David Habgood*

BASINGSTOKE With a background of Wilts & Dorset vehicles of various types, Royal Blue Bristol RELH6G ATA 105B is seen at Basingstoke bus station while operating a London to Plymouth service via Salisbury, Yeovil and Exeter. New in July 1964, ATA 105B was one of a batch of 14 similar coaches received that summer. They had manual gearboxes and were well suited to sustained high-speed running, being easily capable of speeds exceeding 80mph. Subsequently withdrawn at the beginning of 1977, ATA 105B passed to Kendall & Rettalick of Guildford, then to Morris of Swansea. *Brian Jackson*

SALISBURY This coach station just off Castle Street to the north of Salisbury city centre replaced the previous interchange point at Salt Lane for express coaches in the city. The photograph shows two Bristol MW6G coaches awaiting departure to London; in the lead, XUO 734 had been new to Royal Blue in June 1958, while behind it 621 DDV had entered service in March 1960. Notice the direction sign to the City Centre visible on the building in the background; this is a relatively short and very pleasant walk along a footpath beside the River Avon. *Brian Jackson collection*

WEYMOUTH A Bristol RELH6G new to Royal Blue in 1967 nicely illustrates the final version of the traditional-style livery. It was photographed at Weymouth on 23 April 1970 while working a service from Bournemouth to Plymouth via Bridport and Exeter. The 'Mayflower 70' roundel attached to the front of the coach commemorates the 350th anniversary of the sailing of the Pilgrim Fathers from Plymouth to America. This fine coach was withdrawn when only ten years old in 1977. *M. Thresh*

NORTHAMPTON A feature of express coach operation is the considerable variation in the level of customer demand through the various seasons of the year. At busy periods, coaches from the Southern National and Western National fleets were drafted in to help; from the mid-1960s these coaches had been painted dark blue to make them look more in keeping with this role. At the United Counties Bedford Road depot in Northampton on 24 December 1970, suitably liveried Southern National Bristol RELH6G OTA 630G (left) waits to depart with an Associated Motorways service to Bournemouth. Parked alongside, AEL 2B is a Hants & Dorset Bristol MW6G providing a duplicate vehicle, as loadings were no doubt heavy on Christmas Eve. *M. Thresh*

The white years

The National Bus Company came into being from 1 January 1969, and before too long top management was giving thought to a corporate identity for coaches operated by subsidiary companies. In 1970 what turned out to be a fairly short-lived interim scheme was agreed for operators in South West England consisting of white with a broad waist rail in the appropriate fleet colour – on which the fleet name would be shown in white. As it happened, this livery particularly suited a batch of Bristol LH6L coaches fitted with 41-seat Duple bodies that came into service in 1970; the design of the body resulted in a deep waist band and therefore a large area of dark blue. A line-up of these coaches was caught by the camera when newly delivered. *The late David Habgood collection*

DERBY The interim livery scheme certainly did not sit so nicely on the post-1962-style Eastern Coach Works body fitted to Bristol MW coaches; the overall effect was rather bland, as illustrated by 265 KTA, photographed at the Trent garage in Derby ready to work an Associated Motorways journey to Weymouth during the summer of 1971. When a coach thus repainted had first appeared at Bournemouth coach station, an inspector said to one of the drivers, 'See that white coach over there? That's the beginning of the end of Royal Blue.' It was true that the traditional identity was declining, but time was to prove that there is still a healthy market for express coach travel. *Brian Jackson*

TAUNTON AEC Reliance 3MU3RU 938 GTA had been new to Devon General in June 1961, and was fitted with a Willowbrook coach body 7ft 6in wide and seating 41 passengers, being intended for local tours duties along some of the narrow lanes of Devon. Having passed to Greenslades Tours in 1970, 938 GTA came into the Royal Blue fleet in July 1971. The interim-style livery suited this vehicle rather well and, despite the fact that it is rather different from the Bristol/ECW vehicles to which the company's regular passengers had become accustomed, there was no doubt that this was a Royal Blue coach. Here it is seen proceeding eastwards out of Taunton, operating an express service bound for Yeovil. Subsequently withdrawn in 1973, 938 GTA went for scrap at Plymouth in December of that year. *Brian Jackson*

DERBY Bristol LH6L RDV 446H, carrying a 41-seat coach body by Duple, is seen at Derby bus station ready to work an Associated Motorways journey to Weymouth. The driver, Steve Bousfield, is looking, perhaps somewhat wistfully, at the Midland General Bristol RELH6G that has pulled in behind his coach. Seen here operating the MX 4 service to London, 1386 R carried a 51-seat dual-purpose body by Eastern Coach Works, and had been new to Midland General in May 1964; it remained in that fleet until April 1977. This bus station in Derby had opened in 1933 and was built to a design very much of its period; it was subsequently closed in October 2005, and a replacement was provided a few years later as part of the Riverlights development. *Brian Jackson*

BLAKENEY This photograph illustrates how versatile Royal Blue and Associated Motorways drivers had to be at times when peak loadings led to emergency situations. Brian Jackson was working a Saturday-only Weymouth-Cheltenham-Derby journey when he was redirected at Cheltenham to take over instead a Cheltenham to Porth service, a route that wound its way through the South Wales valleys and required good geographical knowledge. The following morning, Sunday 28 May 1972, Bristol LH6L RDV 446H was photographed at Blakeney, still with the Porth sticker in the windscreen, while returning to Cheltenham ready to work an afternoon duplicate back to Weymouth. *Brian Jackson*

WINCHESTER A nationwide standard National Express livery was introduced in 1973. It was all-over white, with the 'National' corporate identity in alternating red and blue letters, and the company fleet name in smaller red capital letters over the front wheel arch. As the coaches were progressively repainted in this style, the Royal Blue fleet became Royal Blue in name only. But while many were saddened at the loss of the old traditional colours, it must also be said that the bold step to go for the white livery that would be seen (and instantly recognised) in all parts of the country was exactly the right move at the time; it successfully emphasised the message that National Express truly was national. Bristol RELH6G 394 TUO, in service with Royal Blue from June 1964 until December 1977, had recently been painted in National Express livery when photographed at Winchester while working route 700 to London. *Brian Jackson*

BOURNEMOUTH During the early hours of Sunday 25 July 1976 the two-tier bus and coach station in Bournemouth was devastated by a blaze so fierce that a ship crossing Poole Bay radioed ashore to ask about the strange light that could be seen over Bournemouth. The seat of the fire was on the lower level, and this photo, taken a few days later, illustrates the scene of complete destruction that had previously been Bournemouth coach station. A number of coaches parked on the lower level were reduced to virtually unrecognisable pieces of twisted metal. From that morning the National Express coach terminal in Bournemouth was transferred to the Shamrock & Rambler garage in Holdenhurst Road, where it remained until Bournemouth Travel Interchange was opened beside the town's railway station in November 1988. *Brian Jackson*

BOURNEMOUTH This Plaxton-bodied Bristol RELH6L coach had been parked at the foot of the entry ramp into the coach station on the night of the conflagration, and suffered heat and smoke damage rather than being completely destroyed. Several days later it was hauled back up the ramp and into Exeter Road prior to being towed by the AEC Matador recovery truck to Rutland Road for attention. Quite apart from the coach being smoke-blackened, various plastic and rubber fittings, including the window seals, had melted. Nonetheless, the coach was repaired and re-seated, and returned to service the following year. In 2017 the BH2 complex of cinemas, cafes and restaurants stands on the site formerly occupied by the bus and coach station. *Brian Jackson*

WEYMOUTH Two Bristol RELH6G coaches in National Express white livery are seen awaiting departure from Weymouth. On the left, RDV 425H, new to Royal Blue in 1970, is on route 723 to London. Perhaps of greater interest is the coach on the right; in October 1963 861 UAE had been the first production Bristol RE coach to be delivered to the Bristol Omnibus Company, and had been one of a batch of 19 RE coaches transferred from that company to Royal Blue in 1974. By the time this photograph was taken, all Royal Blue coaches were operating in National Express white livery. *Brian Jackson*

TAUNTON Following a decision made in 1986 that National Express coaches would no longer carry individual company fleet names above the front wheel arches, all of the Royal Blue names had disappeared within the next two years. However, in 1992 the Taunton-based operation that had revived the Southern National name decided to repaint Bristol RELH6G RDV 419H into traditional Royal Blue livery, and in this guise it was used on duties including express work based at Taunton until withdrawn from service in June 1994. Therefore, technically at least, this vehicle had the honour of being the very last coach in Royal Blue livery to operate on normal scheduled express service. *Brian Jackson*

Relief Coaches

RADIPOLE The fact that many people take their holidays from Saturday to Saturday, linked with an inevitable increase in demand for travel during school holiday periods, meant that Royal Blue had to cope with many additional people wishing to travel on summer Saturdays. To cater for these peaks in demand, the first call for Royal Blue was on the coaches used by Southern National and Western National for local tours and private hire work. The years just after the Second World War, when a general shortage of vehicles was matched by a huge demand for travel, saw a number of relatively elderly coaches pressed into service as Royal Blue reliefs. Dennis Lancet I JT 3055, with a 32-seat Duple body, had been new to Greyhound Coaches of Weymouth in 1935, and had been acquired by Southern National with the Greyhound business in 1936. It was photographed at Radipole garage, Weymouth, having just operated a Royal Blue relief journey on a busy post-war Saturday. Subsequently it was withdrawn by Southern National in October 1949, passing to Beacon Tours of St Austell until broken up in 1953. *Brian Jackson collection*

LONDON In addition to Southern National, Western National and other Tilling operators, coaches were also hired from a number of independent operators on summer Saturdays. Gayton's Coaches of Ashburton, Devon, often provided relief coaches between the Torbay resorts and London. Seen at Victoria coach station in the early 1950s was the company's 1949 Commer Avenger LUO 414, which carried a 32-seat centre-entrance body by Plaxton. Passengers who have travelled from south Devon will have enjoyed a comfortable, if rather noisy, journey on this coach. *Roger Grimley*

YEOVIL The hiring in of extra vehicles on summer Saturdays was still widespread in the late 1960s. Neighbouring Tilling group operator Wilts & Dorset so often provided vehicles for this purpose that 'On hire to Royal Blue' was included in its destination blinds. This is demonstrated by Bristol MW6G EMR 300D, new in 1966 and carrying a 39-seat dual-purpose body by Eastern Coach Works, which was caught by the camera during a refreshment break at Yeovil. These dual-purpose vehicles served Wilts & Dorset well, being used variously for tours and excursions, forces leave express services, Royal Blue relief work, and on occasion ordinary local bus services. *R. H. G. Simpson*

LONDON When every available coach is being used on a summer Saturday, problems can arise if a vehicle breaks down. On this occasion in 1971 the coach that had worked the 09.00 service from London to Weymouth was found to be unable to provide the scheduled return journey after arrival at the Dorset resort. The only substitute vehicle available was a new 53-seat bus, Bristol RELL6G UTT 560J. It was photographed at Victoria coach station, having made an excellent run up from Weymouth, but being a bus it was sent back empty to its home depot. *Brian Jackson*

LONDON Very occasionally unforeseen circumstances such as a breakdown or serious traffic delay could lead to an unusual vehicle being provided for a relief journey, as can be seen on this occasion in 1971. KEL 408 had been new to Hants & Dorset in July 1950 as a Bristol L6G coach carrying a 28-seat Portsmouth Aviation body. In 1961 the coach body was removed, the chassis lengthened to 30 feet and the engine replaced by a six-cylinder Bristol AVW unit; a new 39-seat Eastern Coach Works bus body was then fitted, and KEL 408 became a driver-only-operated Bristol LL6B bus in April 1962. It was transferred from Hants & Dorset to Wilts & Dorset in August 1970. Normally it was used on more local duties, but this stint as a Royal Blue relief showed that the by then elderly vehicle was still capable of spirited running – apparently it overtook the service car, and beat it into London's Victoria coach station by a comfortable margin. This was, however, something of a swansong for KEL 408; it was withdrawn from service in July 1972. *Brian Jackson*

After Royal Blue service

LISKEARD The influx of Bristol MW coaches into the Royal Blue fleet saw a number of the older Bristol L types transferred to the Western National and Southern National fleets to be rebodied as driver-only-operated buses. This was achieved by lengthening the chassis to 30 feet and fitting a new Eastern Coach Works bus body. In this way 26 vehicles were converted from Royal Blue coaches to ordinary local buses, which went on to give very good service in the West Country. A typical example was JUO 933, new in 1948, which had its original 31-seat Beadle coach body replaced by a 39-seat Eastern Coach Works bus body after coming off Royal Blue service in 1958. It is seen awaiting its next turn of duty at Liskeard railway station on 11 June 1966. *Brian Jackson*

BOURNEMOUTH For many years the outstanding reliability and standard of presentation that was a noted feature of Royal Blue coaches maintained at the Rutland Road premises in Bournemouth was overseen by Mr John Horn, Engineering Superintendent (Royal Blue), then Area Engineer at Bournemouth. It had been Mr Horn's wish that a Royal Blue coach should follow the cortège to his funeral; consequently on 4 September 1985 this preserved Bristol LS6G, then in the care of the Dorset Transport Circle, carried past and present company managers to Bournemouth crematorium on this sad occasion to pay their final respects to this very popular man. *John Taylor*

FIDDINGTON In 2017 the distinctive Royal Blue livery is no longer seen on the regular express coach services to the West Country, but we are fortunate indeed that a number of former Royal Blue coaches have been preserved and often attend running days in various parts of the country, reminding us of times gone by. Two preserved and beautifully maintained examples, Bristol LL6B LTA 729 and Bristol LS6G OTT 98, are illustrated on the front cover of this book. It takes great dedication and considerable cost to restore a vehicle to that standard. An idea of the challenges that preservationists face is provided by this photograph of former Royal Blue coach RU 8805, as it was when discovered in a field. The preservation of this AEC Reliance, which was new to Royal Blue in March 1929, is of particular significance as it is the only remaining vehicle from the days when Royal Blue was owned by Elliott Brothers; it is carrying the replacement 28-seat Beadle coach body it was given in 1936 and which it used in service until 1950. The Thames Valley & Great Western Omnibus Trust is now undertaking the restoration of this fascinating survivor.

I hope you have enjoyed *Royal Blue Recollections*, and that you will have a chance to see, and perhaps travel on, a preserved Royal Blue coach at a rally or running day before too long, so that you can really soak up the atmosphere of days gone by. *Colin Billington*

Index

ROYAL BLUE
SERVICES
Summer
1952
TIME TABLE
3d
Commencing 7th April, 1952 until 19th October, 1952 (inclusive).
Cancelling issue dated 22nd October, 1951.